how to be a

Fashion designer

Written by Lesley Ware

Dolls by Tiki Papier

Penguin Random House

Written by Lesley Ware
Illustrator Tiki Papier

Project editor Satu Fox
Editorial assistant Megan Weal
US Senior editor Shannon Beatty
Americanizer Mindy Fichter
Senior designer Joanne Clark
Designer Emma Hobson
Additional design Ala Uddin, Rashika Kachroo
Jacket designer Elle Ward
DTP designer Vikram Singh
Managing editors Deborah Lock, Laura Gilbert
Managing art editor Diane Peyton Jones
Pre-production producer Dragana Puvacic
Producer Barbara Ossowska
Art director Martin Wilson
Publisher Sarah Larter
Publishing director Sophie Mitchell

First American Edition, 2018
Published in the United States by DK Publishing
345 Hudson Street, New York, New York 10014

DK books are available at special discounts when purchased in bulk for
sales promotions, premiums, fund-raising, or educational use. For details,
contact: DK Publishing Special Markets, 345 Hudson Street, New York,
New York 10014 SpecialSales@dk.com

Printed and bound in China

All images © Dorling Kindersley Limited
For further information see: www.dkimages.com

A WORLD OF IDEAS:
SEE ALL THERE IS TO KNOW

www.dk.com

CONTENTS

Hi, I'm Lesley. I write books about fashion, teach sewing classes, and design (all the time).

To future fashion designers...

I am so excited that you have this book in your hands. You are at the beginning of your journey into fashion!

This book will help you learn the skills of fashion design. Fashion is a fun way to express your personality. I always say that if you can speak up with fashion, you can speak up in other ways, too.

You will also discover how to be a stylist. While designers create the clothes, stylists know how to put them together. They choose clothes for photo shoots and dress people for dazzling events.

Last but not least, designers need to care about the environment. This book will help you think about how you shop and inspire you to give old clothes new life.

Enjoy the magical fashion-filled journey ahead!

This is my kitten, Miles Ware. He likes to help me sew, but makes a mess of my threads! He wants to become the world's first cat supermodel.

xo, Lesley

Challenge yourself!

Where you see a star, I've set you a designing or styling challenge. Don't worry if you find these tricky or make a mistake. Doing things you find difficult helps you learn. It's part of being creative!

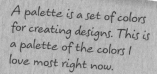 

A palette is a set of colors for creating designs. This is a palette of the colors I love most right now.

I enjoy listening to music when I design and sew!

Drawing

Fashion designers share their ideas through their drawings. Sketch every day, even if it's just for ten minutes. There's paper you can draw on at the back of the book, starting on page 76.

My top tips

Where you see my signature glasses, I've given you handy hints about how to improve your designs, or just fun things to do.

Make it

You'll find great projects throughout the book to help you get started with the practical side of creating real-life fashion.

⚠️ Some of the steps in this book require adult permission. Also, always ask for help from an adult when cutting and sewing since scissors and needles are sharp.

Don't forget!

☆ There is no such thing as "I can't" or "it's ugly"—work until it feels right. Designing is an art, not a science.

☆ Take your time. Have fun with your projects and see where they take you.

☆ Believe in your ideas and follow your instincts. Now—let's get started!

TOOLS

Here are some tools you will need to do the activities in this book. These items, along with a stash of fabric, are a blast to draw and design with. You can also start a library of fashion books to use as inspiration.

Double-sided tape

Mini pom-poms

Sequins

Embellishing

Embellishing is a big word that simply means "decorating." You can easily make your clothes look completely different by embellishing them with pom-poms or sequins.

Colored pencils

Washi tape

Washi tape is sticky tape made of paper. Use it to embellish clothes and decorate mood boards.

Fabric paint

Fabric glue

Drawing

Sketching clothes is fun and you will get better and better if you practice every day. Try different sized sketchbooks and aim to fill the one you like most.

Sketchbooks

Pencil

Crayons

Colored markers

Use thin and thick markers to draw delicate details or chunky stripes.

Scissors

Buttons

Needle

Sewing

To start sewing, you just need a needle and thread. As you start to sew more, you can add more stuff to your kit.

Cotton thread

Dressmaker's pins

Swatches

You can mix dyes to create unique colors.

Fabric dye

Fabric pen

How to do a running stitch

The running stitch is the most common stitch. Think of it as a wave that goes up and down, in and out of the fabric.

Patches

Push one end of the thread through the eye of the needle. Tie a knot in the other end of the thread.

1

When you're finished, tie a knot in the thread to stop it coming loose.

2

Starting from the back, poke the needle through the fabric until the knot stops it moving. Then poke the needle back through the fabric.

Keep moving the needle forward and backward through the fabric. Try to keep your stitches the same distance apart.

3

How to
MOOD BOARD

A mood board is a collection of things that you can use for style inspiration. Fashion designers use them to show their ideas to others. Let's spark new ideas with a rainbow mood board.

Find inspiring things

After you grab a pair of scissors, hunt around for things to add. You can use torn-out pictures, photos, stickers, leaves, and fabric. Try pinning your inspiration to a bulletin board, sticking it to a piece of cardboard, or make a mini-mood board in a sketchbook.

rainbow

Colors

Get started by thinking of a color you like to wear. Look everywhere for inspiration to add to your board, from photos to buttons. Use as many different shades of your color as you can find.

Fabric swatches

Pin inspirational things to your board.

Ask for a few fabric swatches the next time you are at a fabric shop.

Add small objects such as patches or hair clips to your mood board.

Keep an eye out for things that remind you of your mood board colors or theme.

Themes

A theme connects images together. It could be a set of objects such as "cute dogs," or a feeling such as "joy." Make a mood board with a theme that sends a message about your sense of style.

Bracelets

Magazine cuttings

Tear out inspiring quotes from magazines.

Find your voice as a designer

COLOR

Color is the most important element of design because it's part of every single thing you wear. For each collection, fashion designers create a color palette by picking out a few colors that go together.

Blues are cool and serene. They come in lots of tones, from sky blue to navy.

Purples

Pastel blue

Pastels

Pastels are milky, washed out tones that create a soothing effect. They are great for spring outfits.

Lilac

Pinks and reds

Pastel pink

Shocking pink

Pistachio green, lilac, and baby blue are all pastels.

Ribbon is a great trim. Buy lengths of ribbon in a mix of colors for using in projects.

10

Blues and black

Designers love black because it goes with everything.

Teal

Neon pink and sunshine yellow are examples of brights.

Brights

Brights are strong, bold colors. They are fun to wear and look flashy, especially when you wear at least two together.

Color code your fabric to easily see different textures and prints.

Mint green

Sunflower yellow

Yellows and greens

Red, orange, and yellow colors are warm and bright.

👓 Top tip

Contrasting colors are opposites on the color wheel. They stand out strongly when you put them together. Try designing a color-blocked outfit in contrasting tones.

Color wheel

Balloons

Design an outline using the shape of a balloon. Try a ballooning sleeve, dress, or pants.

Flag garland

Deep purple

Green

Blue

Create a new mood board using this carnival color palette.

Circus tent red stripes

Ferris wheel

ADMIT ONE

Tickets

Cotton candy

At the CARNIVAL

Carnivals are an unlimited source of inspiration. Pick a carnival-themed word to inspire your design—think of things like happy, light, star, candy, or neon.

Let the sights, sounds, and even tastes and smells of the carnival inspire you. Can you design a popcorn-inspired look?

Popcorn

Be inspired by the colors and **stripes** of the big tent.

Masquerade mask

Circus tent

Stars are the symbols of performers.

12

The look

This look is for the girl that is ready to slay all day, checking out the amusements that come her way! No need to be plain when you can look like a star.

A flag-patterned scarf keeps this girl's hair from blowing around on all the fairground rides.

Circus-tent stripes make a cute T-shirt pattern.

How can you include light in your designs? Consider reflective materials, LED lights, or glow-in-the-dark paints.

Bright lights

This bracelet has chunky sections shaped like fairground tickets.

Add studs or gems to your design in a shape you adore. This girl just loves shining stars.

A cuffed jumpsuit looks summery. You can make your own rolled-up cuffs by fixing with a few stitches.

Juggling clubs

Create a cool and quirky look fit for a juggler, but easy to wear every day.

Wearing comfy shoes is a must at the carnival. She can't have fun if her feet are hot.

Pick a PALETTE

Color is one of the most powerful and popular elements of fashion design. Check out these looks for different ways that designers use color. Then create a personal palette by choosing a set of colors that works well for you.

⭐ ## Challenge

Create a color-blocked, a pastel, and a crazy color look from what you already have in your wardrobe. Lay each outfit on your bed or a clean floor so you can clearly see whether it works or not. This is just the first draft of your look! Keep swapping in items until it is perfect. Don't forget to include shoes (see pages 34–35) and bags (see pages 24–25).

Confident color-blocking

A statement necklace in a matching color makes the look even stronger.

Dark pants are great for color-blocking as they contrast well with bright, bold colors.

Color-blocking

On your mark, get set, color block! A color-blocked look means wearing two or more solid-colored pieces of clothing. It's an easy look to achieve by mixing one or two bright colors with a dark one.

Top off your outfit with a frothy hair accessory.

Ice-cream shapes are the ultimate pastel pattern.

Jelly shoes started as a trend in the 1980s and they are still fashionable now.

Color clash

Stick to just two pastels in one outfit to avoid sweetness overload.

Go wild with color-clash shorts, then balance with a plain top.

Ice-cream pastels

Tank top

Sweatshirt

Pastels

Pastels are milky and washed out, like ice cream or a fuzzy dream. Wear pinks, yellows, and baby blue for a soothing set of hues.

Crazy color

If you want to jump out of the box a bit, go crazy with an explosion of color! Ice-dyed pieces (see pages 16–17) are a great way to achieve this look.

ICE-DYED TOP

Fabric dyeing is like watching magic happen before your eyes! There are many different types of fabric dyeing, such as batik or tie dye. Ice dyeing is an easy way to create shapes on fabric.

Essentials

☆ Cotton top

☆ Draining rack

☆ Tray or pan

☆ Ice cubes

☆ Plastic gloves

☆ Plastic spoons

☆ Powdered fabric dye

1 Wet your top and scrunch it up

Place your top on the rack inside the tray. Cover it with lots of ice. Put on plastic gloves and use a spoon to sprinkle dye on the ice. The more you use, the stronger the colors will be.

The powdered dye sinks onto the top as the ice melts.

Use plastic spoons to carefully sprinkle colors onto the ice.

2 Leave the ice to melt

Leave your top for 6–8 hours until the ice is completely melted. Put on plastic gloves before taking the top out of the tray. Using cold water, rinse the top in the sink until the water is clear.

Be careful when pouring away the melted ice.

Top tip

Top tip

Make sure the dye and the fabric you are using work together. If your top is 100 per cent cotton, use a dye for natural fabrics. Synthetic (man-made) fabrics need special dyes.

3 Your new ice-dyed top

Wash your top in the washing machine (on its own). Leave it to dry and enjoy your new top! Next time, try mixing the powdered dyes together before sprinkling them on and see what colors you can create.

The finished result!

If you love the watercolor-style patterns, make one for your best friend.

If you live in a cold area, try this project using snow!

Style SEEKER

True style is as much about what you do as how you look. Do you love to run, read, draw, or sing? Design an outfit for each activity. Try out each style to find one you feel comfortable in, or invent your own.

Chilling

Try this boho look while painting, writing, inventing new recipes, or just hanging out in the garden.

Find tough textures for a grungy look.

Wear dreamy flower accessories.

Dark, glowing colors add glamour.

Performing

This could be the perfect style for you if you love to perform, model, dance, or go to shows and musicals.

Creating

This could be a good look for you if you skate, explore, or create music. You might like to work behind the scenes on a play, or go camping.

Challenge

In this space, write a list of the things you love to do. Turn the list into a story or poem about your personal style.

I love to...

Moving

This is a cool but practical style for running, hiking, playing sports, going on bike rides, or any other outdoor activity.

Sporty fabrics are light and easy to move around in.

Sing, race, dance, invent

Cook, draw, swim, chat, explore

Create your own pattern with paper shapes. Cut out lots of shapes and stick them down. Photocopy onto transfer paper to add your pattern to a T-shirt.

Can you create a print in your sketchbook using this palette of colors?

Fuchsia

Burnt orange

Aquamarine

Designing
PATTERNS

Fashion designers often work with patterns, also called prints. Designing patterns is a whole job in itself. You have to know all about color and use creativity. Use patterns in your designs for an easy way to create an instant impact.

Plaid is a traditional pattern that is also used in 90s-style grunge fashion.

Plaid

Novelty prints will get people talking.

Fruity

Checked

Gingham pattern is a type of **check** made up of two sets of stripes.

This type of floral fabric is known as toile. Toile means "cloth" in French.

Striped

Floral

The look

Fashion alert! This outfit is for the girl who is bold and not afraid to mix and match her prints. She is a free thinker, who loves to express herself. Similar colors help balance clashing patterns.

Wrap up with a printed **plaid** scarf.

Raspberry pink

Teal

Stay warm with a **checked** overcoat in a classic cocoon shape.

Rotating the pattern on the pockets makes them stand out.

A cube bag hangs on the hip for a relaxed style.

👓 Top tip

You don't have to go for pattern overload. Try adding a checkerboard patch to your pants, wearing a pair of striped tights, popping on a polka-dot beanie, or covering up with a floral jacket.

Floral-patterned pants make a bold statement.

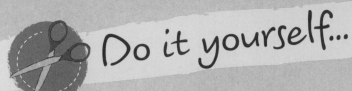

PRINT YOUR OWN PATTERN

Stamping a pattern onto fabric lets you create a cool print while showing off your artistic side. Buy pre-made rubber stamps at a craft store or use everyday objects from around the home to make your own stamps.

Essentials

☆ Things to stamp with: sponges, leaves, or shop-bought stamps

☆ Paper for practicing

☆ Fabric ink or paint

☆ Plain cotton fabric

☆ Iron

☆ Fabric pens

Sponge shapes

1 Make a stamp
There are plenty of household objects that get the stamp of approval. Sponge or paper can be cut into any shape you like, or rolled up tightly to create a rose print. Or you can buy cute rubber stamps.

Rubber stamp

Fabric paint

2 Design your pattern
Test your print by creating a pattern on paper. Press the stamp firmly into the ink or paint so it is covered completely, and then onto the paper. Take time to figure out which shapes you like the most.

Test out different color combinations.

Create an artist's palette of different colors.

22

3 Stamp a patterned fabric

Now stamp your design onto fabric. Make sure you are pressing firmly into the ink or paint each time you stamp. Let it dry. Ask for help to iron the fabric, without steam, to lock in the ink.

Collected leaf

Use a fabric pen to add fine details to your print.

The finished result!

For best results with leaf printing, paint directly on the leaf and then press it onto the paper.

Leaf print

Leaves create soft, natural shapes.

Use bottle caps to print circles.

Cut up your fabric to create something cool, such as a scarf.

Rubber stamps are great for more detailed designs.

Ink pad

23

Bag shapes

Pouch

Pouches are handy for carrying things like your toothbrush.

Envelope

Keep your drawings in an **envelope** bag. This color is red hot.

A pretty bag with a chain strap will hold your things while you dance the night away!

Evening bag

Tassels or fringes look great on shoulder bags. Try one in jet black or icy white, or pair with embroidered details.

Fun shapes

Be bold and wear a fruity statement bag. Pineapple is a fashion favorite.

Reflect your style with a shiny shell bag.

IN the BAG

Bags come in many sizes, from tiny to extra-large. Which one you choose depends on what you need to carry around. Imagine you're taking a trip and think about what bags you'd need for your vacation.

Fashion designers usually have a large bag to carry their designs and tools in.

Satchel

Buckle

The **strap** of a satchel can be worn across the body or over the shoulder.

Embroidered straw bags are a laidback choice for summer.

Handbag

The look

This look is for the girl who loves to travel. She's a world explorer! Effortlessly put together, she can hit the road or soar through the skies with her trusty bag on her arm.

Contrast the color of the **strap** with the body of the bag.

A jumpsuit is a comfortable traveling outfit.

You need a large, spacious bag for long trips.

Put small but important things like your passport, earphones, or gum in an **envelope** bag.

Top tip

Did you know there are designers who focus just on bags? Think like a handbag designer and draw the inside of the bag as well as the outside. Include a pocket, a patterned lining, and a label.

OUTLINES

An outline is the shape that an outfit creates when it's worn. Outlines are also called silhouettes. Adding volume to the top or bottom of an outfit creates a new outline. Legendary fashion designer Coco Chanel believed that clothes should follow the line of a girl's body. Check out these outlines to see if you agree.

Boatneck top.

Close-fitting pencil skirt.

Straight silhouette

Change the shape

Belting your outfit can change the shape of your look in a major way. From oversized sweaters to a simple dress, use a belt to create a totally different outline.

Basic shift dress

Pulled in with belt

Balanced

Balanced fashion looks use a straight silhouette. This gives a basic outline that is relaxed and casual, although the look can be bold, depending on the color and texture of the fabric used. This outline was popular in the 2010s.

Puffed-sleeve blouse.

Wide shoulders

High-waisted fitted pants.

Simple halter top.

Full skirt

Full, knee-length pleated skirt.

Top volume

Add volume to your top with big, puffed sleeves for a dramatic yet cool look. This is a modern twist on vintage clothes with shoulder pads. Top-heavy outlines were popular in the 1980s and '90s.

Fuller below

The skirt gets all the volume in this silhouette. Puffy and pleated skirts made from tulle, cotton, or other swishy fabrics are fab and fun to twirl in. This outline was popular in the 1950s and early '60s.

Streamers add movement and color to the party space. →

Use bright balloon colors in a design. What fabrics mimic their texture?

Bright yellow

Sky blue

Juicy orange

Create a party outfit using this outrageous celebration palette.

Ready to PARTY!

Parties are a ball! We get to show off our sparkling side and have fun. Each season has reasons to celebrate, like your birthday or the end of the school year. So, twirl around and dance on the inside while you plan out what you'll wear. Where will this amazing party dress take you?

Try pastels for a sweet twist on bright colors.

Birthday cake

Use sequins that look like cake sprinkles on your designs.

Cake pop

Find the contrasting colors in these candies and use them to design a palette.

Use the eye-catching colors of presents as inspiration, then top your design with a **bow**.

Mint
green

Hot pink

The look

Stand out at the party in a fierce and unforgettable outfit. This girl is not afraid to go all out to make herself memorable. Whether the party is an arty gathering, or a glittering disco, she thinks like a fashion superhero.

Chandelier earrings are great when you want to feel most special.

What texture would your party dress have? Silky fabrics create a shining surface.

This girl's dress is decorated with a huge sky-blue and yellow **bow** for maximum impact.

Embellish the skirt with trim to look like a layered **birthday cake**.

Bright blocks of **candy**-inspired color are perfect for a celebration.

Love your DENIM

Denim is the best fabric to DIY because it's sturdy, making it easy to cut and embellish just the way you like. Design a denim jacket that matches your style, or challenge yourself to try a totally new denim accessory!

Light or dark?

Denim is described as being a light or dark wash. Try both on to see which you prefer.

Light denim

Embellishments show up better on light wash.

Dark denim

Dark wash is classic and goes with everything.

One jacket, three ways

In your sketchbook, write at least three steps that you will take to complete a jacket redesign. This is your process. Successful fashion designers always have a process so it's good for you to have one too.

Add patches

Play around with where you place your patches. Go with the ideas that pop out at you!

Some patches can be ironed on, or you can sew or safety pin them on.

Denim all over

Denim is always popular because it truly fits any style. Here are a few items you might wear with your awesome upcycled jacket.

Overalls

After cutting, you can fray away (see page 33) to create a textured edge.

Snip the sleeves

If the sleeves on your jacket are not working for you, give them a snip (but ask permission first). A denim vest looks stylish over long-sleeved tops.

If you decide to sew by hand, use a tiny running stitch (see page 7).

Cover the back

Cover the back of your jacket with a piece of fabric by cutting it to fit. Then machine or hand sew it on.

Stitch on a few tassels to make your jacket extra fancy.

Bag

Try adding some patches to a light denim backpack.

Skirt

Frayed shoe bows give an edge to your denim outfit.

Shoes

Denim caps are great for adding a pop of denim to an outfit.

Hat

31

Do it yourself...

DESIGNER DENIM

Let's take a moment to rethink denim. Denim is a strong cotton fabric that is usually blue. It can be used for all sorts of clothing, such as overalls, skirts, and (you guessed it) jeans! Grab the materials that you'll need and get creative.

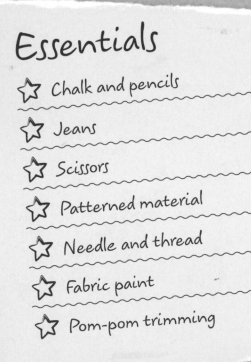

Essentials

☆ Chalk and pencils

☆ Jeans

☆ Scissors

☆ Patterned material

☆ Needle and thread

☆ Fabric paint

☆ Pom-pom trimming

1 Mark your design
Use chalk or a pencil to draw the shapes that you want on your jeans. Try on the jeans before you cut them to make sure the shapes are in the right places.

2 Add fabric
Cut out a fabric shape just a bit bigger than the hole you've made. Turn the jeans inside out, then sew on the shape using a running stitch (see page 7) so it covers the hole.

3 Outline with paint
Using fabric paint or a fabric pen, carefully draw around the shapes you have cut, to outline them.

Shiny or colorful fabrics look great with denim.

4 Add trimming

Use a tight running stitch to add a trim to your jeans along the pocket, waistband, or at the bottom of the legs. Be careful with skinny jeans because adding trim might make the leg too narrow for your foot.

The best trims for denim are pom-poms, faux leather, sequins, rickrack, and lace. Decide which you like the most.

Be patient while your fabric paint is drying. Let it set for at least 3 hours before touching.

5 Fray away

Use chalk to mark where you want to fray. Cut the denim into a square or diamond. Use a pencil to gently pull away threads until the shape is frayed at the edges.

Rub sandpaper along the edge to create a distressed look.

Top tip

Thrift stores are secondhand shops where donated clothes are resold at low prices. These are good places to find denim to redesign. Take a trip to shop for jeans or just to get ideas!

33

Types of shoes

Wedge sandal

Go for solids or small dots when choosing your summer sandal "solemate".

Ballet flats

Easy to fit, and to slip on, these are stars among shoes.

Mary Janes

Mary Janes have a strap to keep your feet secure.

Loafers

Wear a loose dress with a pair of moccasin loafers for a free-spirited look.

Sneaker

The athletic craze started in the '80s. Sneakers are now an everyday part of fashion.

Lace-up boot

These boots have comfortable **rubber soles**. You can wear them with almost anything.

Rain boot

Rain boots were originally made of leather but are now made from rubber. Much dryer!

WALK with STYLE

Looking down at comfortable, cute shoes brings great joy. It's like your feet are smiling back at you! Click your heels together and get to know these different types of shoes. Pair yourself with the shoe shape that suits your style and helps you explore the world around you.

Socks with sandals can be a strong fashion look. Try patterned knee-high socks with sandals in fall and spring.

Rollerskates come in all colors and patterns to match your look. Be safe and have fun rolling on by.

Flip-flops

These easy-to-wear shoes should be kept for the beach or pool. Never sew or ride a bike in them!

Top tip

Turn a shoebox into a "cute box." Decorate a box with colorful paper to keep art supplies and inspirational things in.

The look

This girl is ready to walk with style down the streets, or jump into the long grass in her comfy lace-up boots, tights, and thick, slouchy socks. This look rocks!

Chunky **socks** layered over rainbow tights give a punky but cute edge.

Think pink with sweet ribbon **laces**.

A hand-painted pattern gives these **lace-up boots** a new dimension.

Swap your **laces** for an easy upgrade. Try a lacy or sparkly pair, or pick a bold color.

These **rubber soles** are great because they stop her slipping. They also last a long time before wearing out.

35

Bring your camera or phone. Snap photos of the sights you find interesting and add your fave images to your mood board.

Sea green

Ocean blue

Red

Look at all the bright colors around you at the beach and use them in your designs.

Use your sketchbook while you're at the beach to draw **wave** shapes.

Rope could be used for bags, a bracelet, or other accessories.

Rope

At the BEACH

Going to the beach is an adventure for your senses! The wind on your skin, salt in the air, and stunning views can all inspire you to design and create a whole beach look of your own.

Striped shells

The vibrant color of **coral** brightens up any outfit.

Coral

Collect pebbles

See the patterns in **ice-cream** swirls and a waffle cone

A shell and bead tiara crowns this girl's flaming hair.

A parasol protects the girl's skin, and is the turquoise of a tropical sea.

A gorgeous coral-colored plastic necklace.

The look

This ocean-inspired look includes the colors and shapes of the sea, as well as things you might find at the beach. Add an amazing shell tiara to keep the look high fashion.

A top in light, breezy cotton.

A bracelet made from **rope.**

Be a rock star! Use the color and feel of beach pebbles for inspiration.

The ruffle reflects the flowing shapes of ocean **waves.**

⭐ Challenge

Plan out your beach look— match the colors and patterns of your swimsuit, towel, bag, and hat, and maybe bring a piece of matching fabric to rest and read on.

The pink laces were inspired by raspberry ripple ice cream.

STYLISH SUNGLASSES

You don't have to spend your allowance on a pair of far-out frames! Sunglasses protect your eyes while tying your whole look together. Grab your supplies and get ready to craft. All eyes will be on you—or at least on your cat-eye shades.

Essentials

☆ Sunglasses
☆ Pipe cleaners
☆ Washi tape
☆ Strong glue
☆ Jewels and glitter

Glitter

Washi tape

Glitter paint

Pipe cleaners

To add glitter to your glasses, use a coat of clear nail polish and then sprinkle on your favorite color of glitter.

1 Plan your project
Choose a pair of sunglasses to decorate. In your sketchbook, draw your design. Make notes of all the details, such as shapes, colors, and sparkle.

Sparkle!

Round, retro, or rectangular glasses work best for this project.

Try to match the color of the pipe cleaners to the frames.

👓 Top tip

Protect your sunglasses with a case. Cut a rectangle of thick fabric that is twice the size of your frames. Fold in half, then sew up the long side and one of the ends. Slide in your shades!

2 **Add some ears**
Use pipe cleaners for ears. Shape each ear, then use tape on the sides and in the center to fix them on.

Pearls, rhinestones, and sequins will work nicely here.

3 **Stick on jewels**
Embellish your sunglasses by gluing on jewels or pearls. Space them out as evenly as you can.

The finished result!

4 **Finishing touches**
Make your glasses pop by adding a few finishing touches. Try different patterned tape or paint with glitter nail polish.

Try swapping the chunky diamonds with bright buttons for a kooky look.

Hat shapes

Woolly hat with earflaps

A knitted hat brings texture to a winter look.

Fedora

A fedora has a brim and a dent in the crown (top).

Ears

Hats can be playful! This **straw** hat with ears is the cat's meow.

Beanie hat

Head-hugging and brimless, beanies are really comfy.

Floppy hat

This hat is big and beautiful. Wear it to be noticed but stay mysterious under the brim at the same time.

Beret

A beret is usually made from wool. It's soft and cozy in cold weather.

Baseball cap

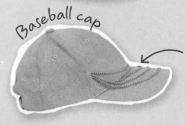

Baseball caps are fun to embellish. Get a plain one and add flowers, chains, or a string of pearls.

HEAD in the CLOUDS

It's okay to have your head in the clouds when you're wearing a hat. If you are a hat person, here are a few shapes to work into your style. Crown your look with the headwear that suits you best.

Top off your look with a tiara. A tiara is a crown with jewels, such as rhinestones.

Summer hat

A summer hat with tassels is perfect for the beach, a summer market, or a street festival.

Adorn your head with a band full of **blossom**.

The look

This girl likes to keep her cool and is always creating a style of her own. A hat and scarf combo is the perfect way to top off a simple outfit. The ribbon and blossoms make the fedora pop, while the patterned scarf frames her face.

Decorate the hat with a ribbon band and **blossom**.

The wide brim of the **straw** hat will help keep the sun away.

To make a **headscarf**, fold fabric in a triangle shape, put it on your head with the fold at the back, and tie a knot at the front.

The bold, bright pattern on this **headscarf** makes the look fashionable and fun.

A T-shirt keeps the look casual by balancing out the fabulous headwear.

Jackets

Add an embroidered patch or appliqué (see pages 46–47) to create original outerwear.

Denim

Bomber

Parka

Dresses

Dresses are great because you can easily make them smart or casual. Try layering one over jeans.

Skimmer

Shift

Striped

SHOP *your* WARDROBE

Before you spend your precious allowance buying more clothes, you should shop your wardrobe! Create new looks by mixing clothes that you've never worn together before. See how it's done with this pink dress.

⭐ Challenge

Get permission and then divide your clothes into three groups:

☆ Too small or short, or you no longer like. Give these away or donate.

☆ Stained or torn but you still like it. These are ready for a makeover (see page 74).

☆ Things to keep, because you love them! This should be the largest pile.

Weekday chic

It may be just a regular day of school, but create a chic and sporty outfit of the day anyway.

One dress that can be worn three ways!

Invest in a backpack you really like since you'll have it all year!

Change laces for a quick customization.

Distressed denim makes an outfit more casual.

Jeans

Leggings

Wide-leg

Bottoms

Hunt until you find the perfect pants. They should be the ideal length to show off your shoes.

Tops

Shirts are super fun to style. Layer sleeveless tops over dresses or shirts.

Tank top

Graphic tee

Button-down

Accessories

Accessories add fun to your outfit. Notice the compliments you get when you wear them.

Headband

Clutch

Backpack

Necklace

Love your denim? Read pages 30–31 for how to embellish your jacket.

Dance-inspired crossed laces

Day out

You are a girl on the go! On Saturdays and school breaks, pull out the special items you rarely wear.

Party time

For a school dance or a family party, pick a look that is playful but comfortable. In winter, swap the shoes for boots.

A statement necklace is all the jewelry you need.

Don't cover it up—let the dress shine!

Matching your bags and shoes looks dressy.

Cardigan

Sweater

Hoodie

Warm Tops

Snuggly sweaters are the perfect layer to wear over any outfit you like.

Sneakers

Flats

Sandals

Shoes

Choose shoes made from material that lets air flow, so you don't get blisters or smelly feet.

Fern

Add leaves to your designs by cutting shapes out of green felt, or stamping them on (see pages 22–23 for pattern printing).

Fuchsia

Fresh green

Mulberry

Create a mood board using this nature-inspired color palette!

Lavender

Petal pink

Lemon yellow

Tropical leaf

Look at NATURE

Let's take a fresh look at nature for inspiration. Use leaves, plants, and flowers to discover amazing color combinations and textures. Are you ready to go hunting for inspiration in the natural world?

Bumpy cactus

 Top tip

Try using the texture of a cactus, or even add spikes to your designs.

Houseplants can be highly stylish! Get an easy-to-grow plant such as a succulent or cactus to bring nature into your room. Have fun developing green thumbs!

Peony

Spiky cacti

Poppy

The look

Turn over a new leaf in this nature-filled, boho look! This outfit is for a girl who loves to stroll around in gardens, or just bring some flower power to the streets of her town.

Silk or plastic **flowers** make great hair accessories.

Sketch your favorite **flowers**, then work them into one of your designs.

A dark background on a pretty floral print top makes the look edgier.

Try a **leaf**-shaped belt buckle.

A strong **green** color shows off these simple, cropped pants.

Flowers are powerful as well as pretty — they grow from tiny seeds into beautiful blooms.

This tote bag has a cute **cactus** and heart appliqué (see pages 46–47).

Wooden clogs keep to the natural theme.

PANDA PATCH

An appliqué is a small piece of fabric sewn onto a larger piece to create a design. Adding an appliqué is a method that fashion designers use to make a basic garment stand out. Create an appliqué for your T-shirt!

1 Draw your favorite animal
Once you've decided on a cool animal, draw it at the size you want your appliqué. Carefully cut out the shapes to create a template for your design.

2 Cut out felt shapes
Trace around the paper template to mark the animal's face onto your fabric. Use small fabric scissors to cut it out.

Ears

Face

Nose

Mouth

Don't forget smaller shapes for the little details.

46

3 Glue the patch together

Use fabric glue to stick the face together. Let it dry for at least one hour. Use fabric marker to add detail to your animal's face.

Top tip

Use paint to create an environment for your animal. Place a piece of cardboard on the inside of the shirt to stop the paint from soaking through, then paint on trees or leaves. Pandas prefer bamboo forests.

The finished result!

Use green paint to draw leaves and plants.

4 Sew on your patch

After the glue is dry on your appliqué, pin it to the T-shirt. Ask an adult for help with this. Then use a tight running stitch (see page 7) to sew on the appliqué.

Challenge

You can use the appliqué process to make a cat, fox, or maybe a jellyfish. You can even add animal pawprints or zebra stripes to your clothes!

WHAT'S
– your –
THING?

Both fashion designers and movie stars often have an iconic style that they've made famous. Maybe they always wear a little black dress or have a signature haircut. They are devoted to the "thing" that makes them memorable. What's yours?

⭐ Challenge

If you don't have a "thing" yet, that's okay! Make a list of the top three items you wear the most. What do they have in common? When you figure out what you like, you're on the path to finding your thing.

Lesley's thing....

I love my **glasses**! When I first got glasses in the 3rd grade, I cried for days because they were big and boring. As I got older, I found frames that I really liked. Now I have five pairs and wear a different color every day. They are like jewelry for my face!

I love my glasses!

I like wearing **denim cut-off shorts** because they are comfortable and you can wear them anywhere—like on vacation in Greece. I've got denim and white versions.

Cool cut-offs

Issy's thing...

Stripes away!

My thing is...

Belle's thing...

I'm into all things nautical. My favorite top is a **striped T-shirt** from France. I wear it with simple, comfortable clothes such as jeans and a pastel-colored raincoat.

TEXTURE

Texture is about the look and feel of materials. Fashion designers add texture to their creations by using a mixture of fabrics and trims. Next time you are looking at fabrics, think about how they feel: which ones are smooth, rough, fuzzy, gritty, or silky?

Tough

Tough fabrics are often heavy and strong. For example, denim was originally worn by men working in construction because it was hard to rip. Tough fabrics are tightly woven, with hundreds of little threads.

Leather is strong and comfortable, but expensive.

Leather

Denim

Denim is always popular because it is smooth and strong.

Scratchy

Scratchy fabrics are often lined with softer fabrics to protect our skin. In some cases, scratchy materials lose their stiffness when they are washed.

Lace

Tulle

Sequined

Sequins are tiny, flat disks made from plastic.

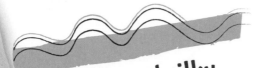

Smooth and silky

Smooth, slippery fabrics make beautiful clothes that are often soft and light. Silk and velvet are perfect for evening gowns.

Challenge

Go to your closet and find at least three textures. Put them together to create an outfit you've never tried before.

Linen

Silk

Velvet

Cotton

Wool

Fake fur

Velvet is smooth because of its pile. The pile is like lots of hairs on the fabric's surface.

Fleece

Light

Light fabrics are thin. These materials are perfect for the summer months because they won't make you sweat.

Warm and fuzzy

Fabrics that are warm and fuzzy are often used to keep us cozy in the cooler months. These fabrics have the most texture of all, as they are made up of chunky fibers woven together.

51

FEELING good

Texture is the feel or surface of a fabric. The feeling of a fabric depends on how it is woven together. Fashion designers are always experimenting with textures and you should too. Try creating contrasts by layering different textures.

Knitted fabric is perfect to wear in the cooler months. Try mixing knitted textures with smooth or metallic ones.

Top this cozy look off with a pretty necklace.

Try out textures

People who work in fashion call the feel of fabric against your skin the "hand" of a fabric. The next time you are in a store or looking in your wardrobe, touch different textures. What is the "hand" of the fabric? Is it soft, rough, crinkly, fluffy, or smooth?

Metallic shoes add a nice polish to your overall look.

Crinkly

Crinkly fabric is fun to wear because it's already crumpled, so you can't mess it up!

Super shiny

Super smooth

Hard, shiny jewelry made from metal or plastic contrasts well with soft sweatshirt material.

Layer a gray sweatshirt with silvery, silky fabrics for an instant texture contrast.

Silky

Silky fabrics are perfect for hair accessories. They slide off easily without damaging your hair.

Layer it on

Start with a simple, basic outfit, then add layers of texture. Layered textures look interesting, and feel even better. Feeling good leads to looking good!

Use a plain outfit as a base.

Fluffy

Slip into fluffy, flat sandals for a casual, textured look.

I love to touch...

I feel comfy wearing...

My favorite textures

What textures do you like best? Write them here or in your sketchbook. Next time you are at a fabric store, ask for samples of these materials to add to your mood board.

Polka dots

Houndstooth

There are so many black-and-white **patterns**—it's fun to mix them up!

Use iron-on photo transfer paper to put a black-and-white photo onto a T-shirt.

Silhouettes

Waves

Curvy

BLACK and WHITE

Designing with black and white is timeless, meaning it never goes out of style. Fashion designers love working with this combination and create all sorts of designs, from peaceful to punchy. Here is some inspiration to get you started.

Show your wild side and take inspiration from zebra **stripes**.

Zebra

Use black-and-white fake fur to give a **panda** vibe to your look.

Add different shaped buttons, in black and white, to your clothes.

Panda

Dalmatian spots are as neat as polka dots. Try using them in your next design.

Dalmatian

The look

This girl keeps it casual and chic by wearing a streetwear look inspired by black and white animals. From snow white to jet-black, fashion magic happens when these opposites attract.

Striped sweaters make a classic statement.

Stack chunky black and white bangles.

Add a **panda** patch or key ring to the bag.

Layer a crisp white shirt under a shorter sweater.

Get a sporty look with striped track pants.

Top tip

When designing with black and white, if you wear a loud top or bottom keep the other clothes simple. For example, wear a plain black or white top with zebra-print leggings.

Checkered slip-ons pack in an extra **pattern**.

Fashion REMIX

Styling with black and white is easy because you cannot go wrong. You will always match when you mix black and white no matter what patterns or textures you add. Try mixing and matching with black and white to create new looks.

SWAP IT!

Patterned

Pop of color

Carry a simple, chic white backpack with black details.

For a fun pop of pattern, swap a plain backpack for a polka-dot black-and-white one.

Black and white is a classic color combination for sneakers.

Shoes are a great way to add a splash of color to your black-and-white outfit.

Instant impact

The same design can look completely different in black or white. A white lace top looks pretty and bohemian, while the same top in black looks more glamorous and gothic.

A (faux) leather jacket is a great way to add a cool edge to your outfit.

Layered

For a pretty, daytime look, try a white top with jeans.

Try a nautical look with a simple, striped T-shirt.

The black version of this top is great if you like an edgy, cool style.

Create a fun, layered look by swapping your T-shirt for a short, pleated dress.

White pants look crisp and fresh. Don't wear them anywhere muddy though!

⭐ Challenge

Try black-and-white dressing for a week! Create looks by mixing prints and solids, going monochrome (one color), and color-blocking. Note down which are your best outfits and why.

Statement

If white pants aren't for you, swap them out for a statement pair of jogging bottoms.

Get in the zone by listening to music on headphones while you are designing.

Bright yellow

Use these colors to create a performance-themed moodboard.

Lime green

Flame red

Headphones

Cool blue

What would soundwaves look like if you could see them?

Zesty orange

Turn up the MUSIC

If you are into fashion you probably love music too! There is a close relationship between fashion and music. Fashion designers need music for their shows and parties, while performers need clothes that will look great on stage. Let music help you develop a rocking look.

Speaker

Electric guitar

Concert

Electric **guitars** come in all sorts of designs, from sunrise orange to traditional wood.

Join the fanclub and be inspired by band T-shirts from concerts or festivals. Concert tees look amazing with denim.

58

The look

This girl's outfit is loud and upbeat, with a fast tempo! The laid-back T-shirt and jeans, combined with lightning-bolt earrings, scream "I'm ready to dance." She'll want to replay this look more than once.

Disco ball

⭐ Challenge

Listen to at least five different types of music, such as jazz, grunge, rock, pop, and hip-hop. Then create an outfit inspired by the music you like best.

This girl always has her **headphones** so she can listen to her playlist.

The silver **guitar** T-shirt was inspired by watching her favorite band live.

A silver chain bracelet will shine like a disco ball.

Decorate your designing space with cute musical tech, such as mini speakers.

This bag was inspired by old-school vinyl records.

Sneakers with studded toes bring in a rocky edge.

Flared disco jeans embroidered with rainbow confetti shapes are perfect for dancing.

59

SPARKLE

A little sparkle goes a long way! Glitter, sequins, and jewels bring drama and magic to your designs. There are no rules to follow when adding these elements into your look. You can pile them on or only use a few. It's up to you.

Try glittery paints to create your own prints and patterns.

Silver and gold

Jewels

Individual jewels are a great way to add some chunky sparkle. Embellish your phone case, tote bag, or even a pair of shoes!

Jeweled phone case

Plan out your placement before you glue to make sure you have enough room.

Glitter reflects the light and comes in a bunch of different colors and shapes.

Sequin trimming

Use a clear thread to sew on your trim for invisible stitches.

Sequins

It's fun and easy to add sequin trim to your clothing to make it sparkle. Use your needle and clear thread to sew into the little holes in the center of the trim.

Rainbow sparkle

Glitter

Nail polish is an easy way to start adding glitter to your look. From there you could try face glitter and temporary glitter tattoos.

Get glitter nail polish in your signature color! Super fun and super you.

Glitter nail polish is tricky to remove. Press a cotton ball soaked with nail polish remover on your nail for 30 seconds before rubbing it off.

Sparkle it up

Try a full-glitter look with clothes, shoes, and accessories. You could even put glitter in your hair. Pile on the glitter and sparkle, then work backward to see if there's anything you want to take off.

A sequined dress always creates a red-carpet moment.

Buy or borrow a stack of bangles. They'll make you feel festive.

Throw all your stuff into a glittery bag and you're ready to go.

Sparkle socks will make your outfit rock.

Be the star that you are in metallic shoes! You can dress them up or down.

GLITZ and GLAM

Now that you understand the basics of sparkle, let's create a casual or dressy look that will fit your style. Let the sidewalk be your catwalk!

A touch of sparkle

If you're not into extreme sparkle, try a T-shirt embellished with jewels or sequins. Throw on a pair of jeans and let the fun begin!

Sequin patches and embellishment give a casual touch of sparkle.

Keep your accessories cute with fun shapes.

Sequins the same color as your outfit will shine in a more subtle way.

Walk like a star with glittery shoes.

Top tip

Make sure you approve of your sparkly look by using a full-length mirror before going out. Which parts are your eyes drawn to? Remember to top it off with a sparkling smile!

Face and hair

In your hair, apply gel where you want the glitter and carefully sprinkle it on. For your face, try stick-on jewels or use eyelash glue.

Finish the look

There are many ways to add glitz and glam to your look. Don't be afraid to dazzle. It's way more fun to look like a movie star than to look at one!

Make glitter tape

Sprinkle lots of glitter on one side of double sided tape. Use it as a temporary trim on your clothes and designs.

Gold is measured in karats. Pure gold is 24 karats.

Silver charm bracelet

Silver

Garnet

Diamond

Ruby

Pearl

Gold

Heart pendant

Amethyst

Adding charms to a bracelet is a good way to celebrate milestones in your life.

Sapphire

Bring on the bling with a statement ring.

Flower ring

Opal

Joyful JEWELRY

Jewelry is both pretty and powerful. Throughout history it has been used for good luck and protection. Wear favorite pieces when you want to calm yourself before a test or you need to feel confident.

Gold chain

Hang your **necklaces** and chains up when you're not wearing them, so they don't get tangled.

Owl brooch

Buy or make your own beaded necklace. Layer different textures and lengths, then show them off by wearing a simple T-shirt.

Brooches are like art you can wear. Pin one on your top, sweater, coat, or even your hat.

Earrings come in many styles, from studs to chandeliers. This pair is for pierced ears but you can also buy clip-ons.

Beaded necklace

Emerald

Peridot

Pick your favorite gem and make it your signature jewel.

Topaz

Aquamarine

Turquoise

The look

Let your confidence shine through with a set of jewels that reflects your personality. Adorn yourself with a few favorites or sprinkle on a lot like this girl. The only rule is to be yourself!

Think outside the box and design a piece of jewelry for your head or feet.

Get a pair of matching friendship bracelets. Give one to a friend to be bracelet buddies.

This girl's signature **earring** shape is a heart. Stars, half-moons, and ice-cream cones are also great shapes.

This statement **necklace** fits her outrageous style. A simple top balances the look.

A **pendant** can be any shape or size, like this huge, colorful bird!

Beaded necklace

Royal blue →

Golden yellow

Use these regal colors to create your Egyptian-inspired look!

Deep red

The Egyptians **pleated** cloth to create dramatic clothing.

Turquoise

Dress like an
ANCIENT EGYPTIAN

Queen Nefertiti was adored for her beauty. She ruled with her husband around 1300 BCE.

Queen Nefertiti

The Ancient Egyptians are known for their rich history, attention to detail, and magnificent style. Combine historic items to create an Egyptian-inspired look. Are you ready to explore the beauty in Ancient Egyptian fashion? Let's travel back in time!

Bracelet

Scarab beetles were the Ancient Egyptians' favorite bugs!

This sculpture of King Tut is made of real gold and precious gems.

Scarab beetle brooch

Sacred eye

Tutankhamun

66

The look

This girl is wearing a softly pleated dress, detailed bomber jacket, and amazing jewelry. Gold was very popular in ancient Egypt. When you create your look be sure to wear golden, copper, or bronze pieces.

Wrap a scarf around your head for elegant **Queen Nefertiti** style.

Adorn yourself with accessories such as gemstone earrings, rings, and bracelets.

The **scarab beetle** inspired this embellishment on a silky bomber jacket.

Regal purple

Golden snake cuff

Channel the regal gowns of the Egyptians with a **pleated** dress.

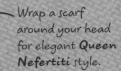

★ Challenge

Plan an Egyptian-themed treasure swap with your friends. Ask everyone to bring a special item to swap. Think gold-colored charms, royal blue nail polish, or gemstone rings!

Keep the look relaxed with knotted slides — or go barefoot.

WRAP up WARM

From cape-like sweaters to star-filled rain jackets, your goal in fall and winter is to stay warm and dry. Use these looks for inspiration and then create a style storm by wrapping up in your own way.

Across seasons

Some days feel too cold to be fall, but still too warm to be winter. These are the perfect times for layering. Try on a cape or a thinner scarf to keep breezes at bay.

Be the star that you are in a patterned raincoat.

A knitted cape will show off your style in a textured way.

Autumn showers

When the cold rain drizzles down, slip into your rain boots, grab your umbrella, pull on a fun printed coat and you'll be just fine.

Find patterned over-the-knee socks or tights that fit your style.

Corduroy is snug when it's breezy outside.

Rain boots come in the coolest prints.

Grab a circle scarf to make your look well rounded.

Fuzzy hats are wonderful and warm. Double pom-poms help you stand out in the crowd.

Light up the fall in lighter colors like cream, beige, and ocher (a warm, spicy yellow). Who says you can't look bright even when it's dark outside? Try designing dramatic coats in all sorts of colors and patterns.

Winter weather

Get the best outerwear by spending plenty of time trying on coats before choosing one. It's worth it, as you'll wear it every day when the skies are gray.

Get a lightweight, yet warm, quilted puffer jacket in a color you adore.

Be dressy but comfortable in a pair of leather slide-in boots.

Cuffed legs keep cold winds out.

Shearling (sheepskin) boots are the best for cozy toes!

PHOTO FABULOUS

Fashion designers need beautiful photos for websites, runway shows, and magazine features. Do a photo shoot wearing something you designed, or were inspired by while reading this book! Use your phone or an instant camera.

How to take great photos

Grab your shutterbug friends and plan your shoot.

Set the mood with music.

Find natural light whenever possible.

Stand up straight.

If you feel awkward close your eyes for a few seconds and think of a happy place.

SMILE (photoshoots don't have to be super serious. Have fun!)

Nature shots

Photos in nature are gorgeous because of the natural light from the sun. Daylight makes photos pretty even if it is shining through the clouds on an overcast day.

Use clouds as a backdrop by getting a friend to snap you from the ground.

Go all natural in nature and let your beauty glow! Frame your face with leaves and branches.

Create a few fun props to use on your shoot. Try flowers, inflatables, or toys.

In the city

Street style photo shoots let you shine in the city. Take to the streets, then use the photos to make a handmade zine or look book for your designs.

In your bedroom

Professional shoots can involve a whole team to make sure everything looks lovely. Recruit a crew, create a DIY backdrop, and get ready for your close up! When shooting indoors, try to use natural light from the windows.

"Composition" is the way you arrange different things in the photo, including yourself.

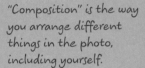

Scout around your neighborhood for locations to use. Look at familiar places in a new way.

Keep an eye out for interesting textures. In the city, this could be bricks, steel, concrete, or stone.

Make a background using streamers. Cut and hang up strips of colored paper.

Create a geometric background using chunky shapes cut out of paper.

A block of color shows off cool textures and outlines. Get a huge sheet of colored paper to use as a backdrop.

Get cosmic inspiration from **space**. Copy the shapes and silvery glow of the moon and stars.

Taupe

Night sky blue

Use this kaleidoscope of nighttime colors to create an out-of-this-world look.

Moon and stars

Soft blue

In your DREAMS

The nights when you get to stay up late and have fun with friends and family are magical and memorable. Check out this inspiration for super cozy bedtime fashion. Sweet dreams!

Twinkly lights

Decorate your room with twinkly lights for a whimsical sleep or work space.

Sleepy polar bear

Pillow fight!

Did you know kittens spend 16–20 hours napping each day? Channel their **fuzzy** fur and relaxed vibe.

Down pillows are made from the feathers of geese and ducks.

Feathers have a mix of straight and fluffy edges.

Top tip

Use a feather, or decorate a piece of card stock with favorites from your art supplies, to make your own bookmarks.

Teal

Heather purple

The look

This cozy look is perfect for a friend's sleepover or a movie night on the sofa with family. When designing your own outfit, keep fabrics soft and snuggly for ultimate sleepwear style.

The contrasting color trim along the edge of this gown is called piping.

Upcycle sleepwear by adding an appliqué, such as this **space-inspired** astrocat (see pages 46–47).

The nightgown is the deep blue of a **night sky**.

Grab a good book and read in bed, or jot down your dreams in a journal when you wake up.

Add deep pockets for treasures, or useful things such as a pencil for writing in your journal.

Think about the season when designing a robe. **Fuzzy** fleece is best for winter, while cotton is best for summer.

Bear-faced slippers keep feet comfy and cozy for midnight snack runs.

73

Do it yourself...

SHIRT RESCUE

You can upcycle clothes that feel a little tired by trying a few clever tricks to improve them. You've learned the running stitch (see page 7). Now gather your sewing kit and that boring shirt you never liked to get started.

Essentials

☆ A boring shirt

☆ Needle and thread

☆ Buttons and fasteners

☆ Fabric scraps

☆ Lace trim

If you don't have matching thread, try a color contrast.

This fastener is called a frog. Frogs are both useful and decorative. Ribbit!

After the makeover!

Before

1 Rethink the sleeves
Roll up the sleeves and fix in place with a fastener (an item that holds clothes closed). If they are too slouchy, hem them with a running stitch.

2 Add a lacy collar
Pin your lace around the collar to make sure it is long enough. Use a running stitch to neatly sew it on, making sure the lace is flat as you go.

This lace trim would also look cute on a T-shirt.

3 Sew on a pocket
Carefully cut a pocket shape out of fabric and stitch it on. Leave the edges frayed or fold them under, depending on how polished you want the shirt to look.

Leave the top of the pocket open so you can tuck away earphones or lip balm.

Sew all the way around your patch to stop the threads unraveling.

4 Swap out the buttons
Replacing plain buttons is the easiest way to perk up your shirt! You could use matching buttons or mix them all up.

Challenge
What types of fasteners could you add to your shirt? The ancient Indus Valley people made buttons from seashells, while modern designers use laces, safety pins, and snaps.

A T-shirt is a blank canvas for you to add your favorite things. Try patterns or drawings based on your favorite food, animal, or activity.

Express yourself
Go wild with doodles on this plain T-shirt.

Use your favorite colors

Use words or phrases in your design.

Hey!

LOL

I love cats

Draw your favorite things

Design a pattern using simple shapes and symbols.

Designers brand their work with logos. Design your own logo by writing your name and adding a symbol.

What trimming would look good on this neckline?

Design your own... PANTS

Create your perfect pants by picking a shape and adding cool extras. Start by drawing on these templates and then create your own designs in a sketchbook.

Trim

Add to the waistband or use to decorate the legs.

Pom-poms

Flowers

Patterns

Do you prefer allover pattern or just in patches?

My pants shape

What shape do you like the best? What activity would you do in these?

Flares

Formal

Baggy

Cargo

Skinny

Copy these shapes into your sketchbook, then add colors and patterns.

Try adding cuffs

Straight leg

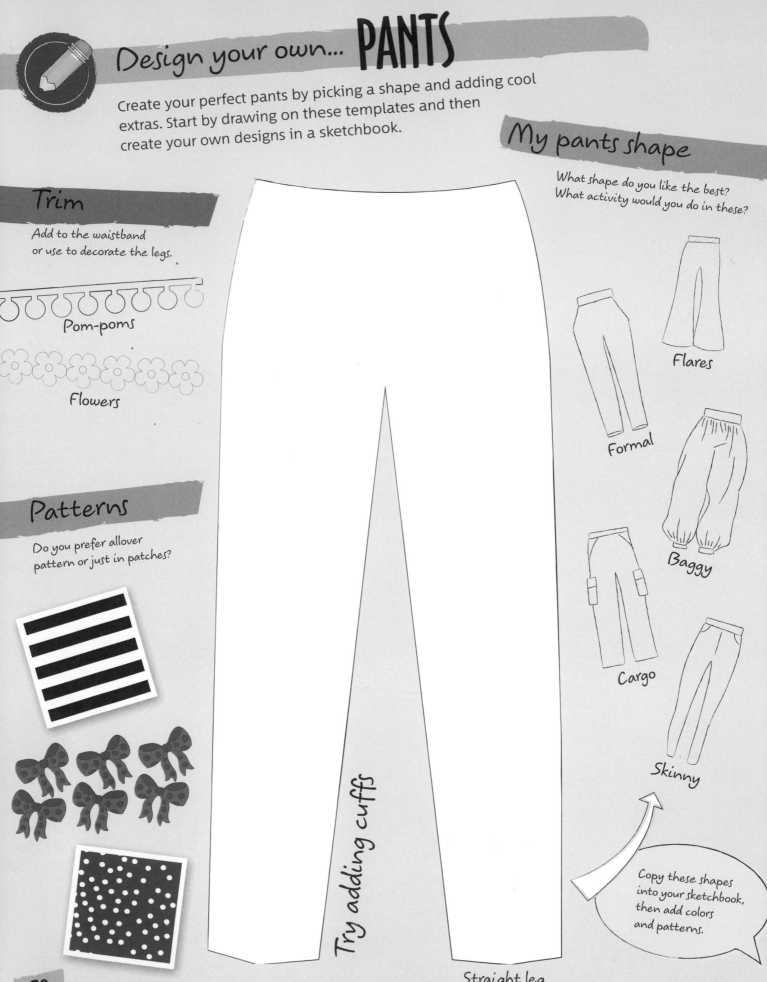

78

Pick any color

Colorful pants make a fashion statement.

Front

Drawing jeans

To make your drawings look like real jeans, use the right details. Color them blue and draw rivets on the pockets.

Try adding some rips and tears.

Add a wide or skinny belt.

Back

Add patches

Design patches inspired by your favorite things.

Design your own... SKIRT

Try out these skirt templates. Once you've chosen a shape, add colours and patterns. What interesting details can you add?

Would you wear this skirt to the park or a party?

Flowing

Invent a fabric

Create a crazy pattern for your skirt (see pages 20–21 for ideas). What pattern works best on floaty or tailored skirts?

Draw on a contrasting seam

Do you want buttons?

Tailored

Pick a pocket

Do you like big or small pockets? Add one to your design.

Could you add a trimming to the waistband?

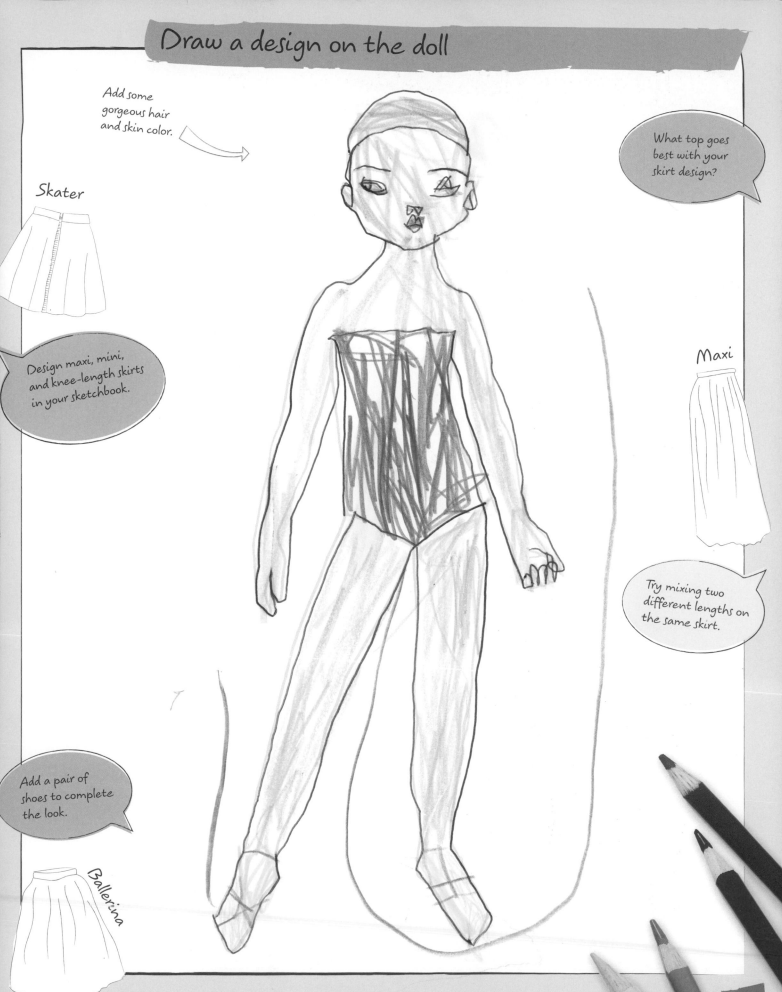

Add some gorgeous hair and skin color.

What top goes best with your skirt design?

Skater

Design maxi, mini, and knee-length skirts in your sketchbook.

Maxi

Try mixing two different lengths on the same skirt.

Add a pair of shoes to complete the look.

Ballerina

Design a... NECKLACE

Necklaces can be tiny and delicate, or large and chunky. Try drawing yourself a nameplate necklace, or design a pendant hanging from a chain in any shape you like.

Draw rows of sequins or beads to design a necklace.

Look at pages 64–65 for ideas.

Test out your design on the doll

Choose sparkling gems or chunky plastic

Design a... HAT

Hats and headdresses are the ultimate way to top off an outfit. Whether you like snuggly beanie hats or fabulous wide-brimmed summer hats, doodle all your ideas here.

Check out the hat styles on pages 40-41 for ideas.

Where would you wear your hat?

Is your hat for winter or summer?

Add some crazy feathers and ribbons.

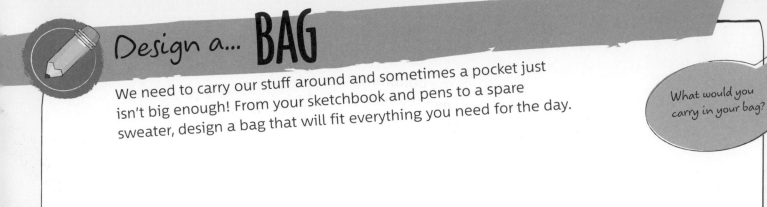

Design a... BAG

We need to carry our stuff around and sometimes a pocket just isn't big enough! From your sketchbook and pens to a spare sweater, design a bag that will fit everything you need for the day.

What would you carry in your bag?

Design an inside pocket and lining for your bag.

How does your bag stay closed?

Look at the bag shapes on pages 24–25 for ideas.

Zip

Buttons

Design some... SHOES

Shoes are made up of the sole on the bottom, the main body of the shoe, and the laces or straps that keep them on your feet. Doodle lots of different combinations to design your own pairs of stylish shoes.

Try different colors on the sole and body.

Design a pattern for the main body of the shoe.

Add a big bow or a dangling tassel to the laces.

Draw some summery sandals (see page 34).

Tassels

Design a pair of cozy winter boots.

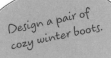

Buckle

Design a... DRESS

A dress can be sporty and casual, or formal and flouncy. Try designing a dress for a day out and one for a party. What makes them different? How would it feel to wear them?

What shape is your dress?

Write down a texture and a color to inspire your dress.

Draw a dream dress

What length is your dress?

Dress to impress

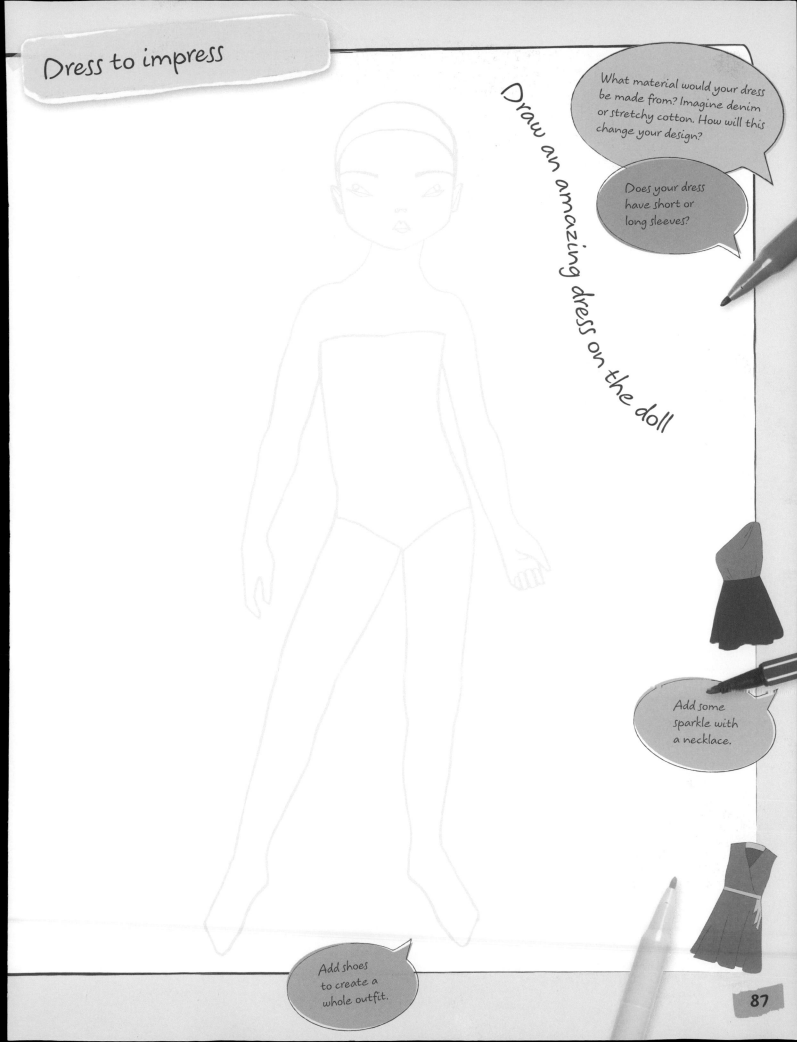

Draw an amazing dress on the doll

What material would your dress be made from? Imagine denim or stretchy cotton. How will this change your design?

Does your dress have short or long sleeves?

Add some sparkle with a necklace.

Add shoes to create a whole outfit.

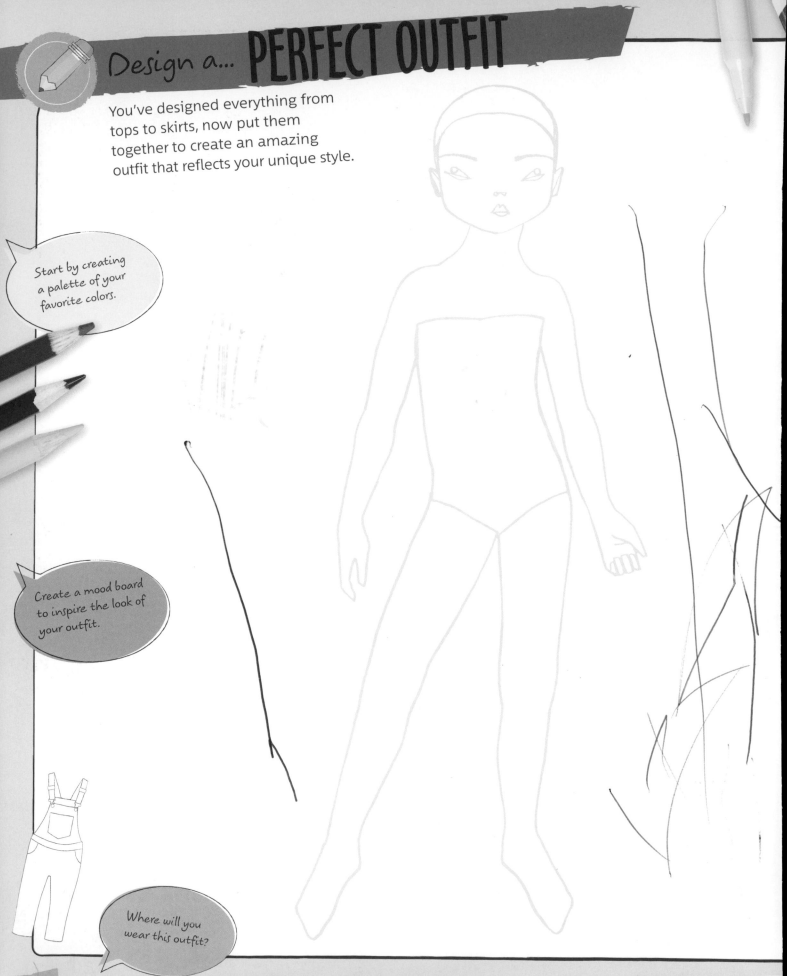

Design a... PERFECT OUTFIT

You've designed everything from tops to skirts, now put them together to create an amazing outfit that reflects your unique style.

Start by creating a palette of your favorite colors.

Create a mood board to inspire the look of your outfit.

Where will you wear this outfit?

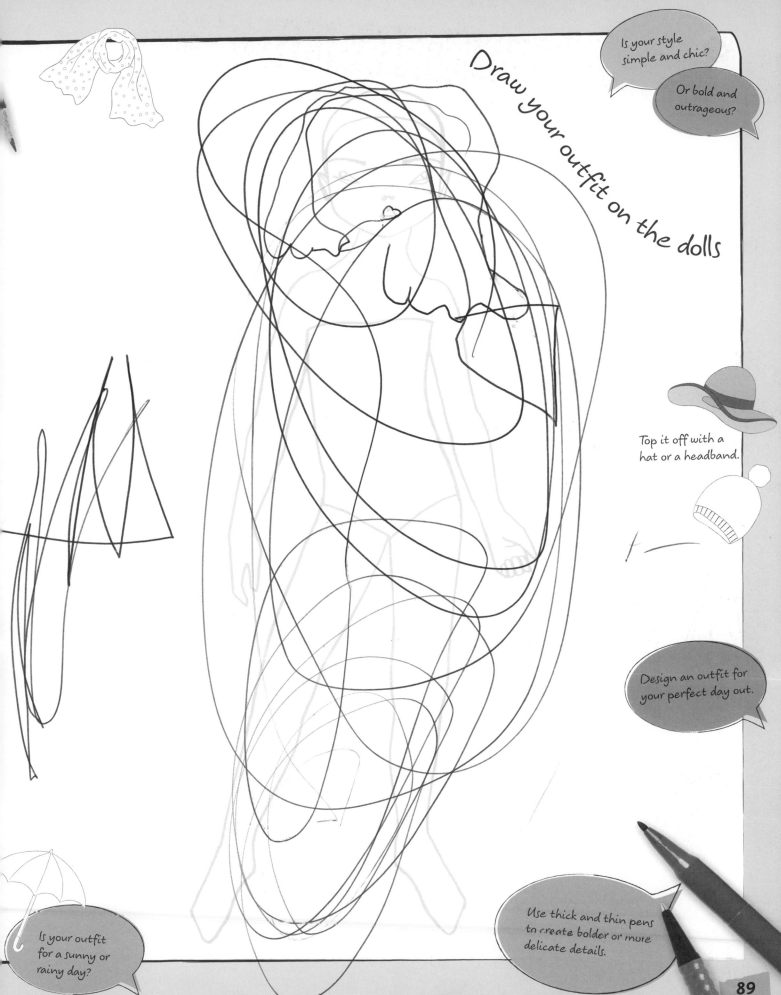

Is your style simple and chic?

Or bold and outrageous?

Top it off with a hat or a headband.

Design an outfit for your perfect day out.

Is your outfit for a sunny or rainy day?

Use thick and thin pens to create bolder or more delicate details.

89

Shorts, skirts, pants, dresses, jumpsuits, jeans, T-shirts, or blouses? Mix them together to draw the outfits of your dreams.

Take a look back through the book if you need inspiration.

Shorts, sk

Add a coat or jacket as a finishing touch. Check out pages 68–69 for coat ideas.

MEt
HAS
SUM
MEIW
C

Let your imagination run wild

Try top-heavy and bottom-heavy outlines.

What's your inspiration?

Practice outlines before drawing them on the doll (see pages 26–27 for basic silhouettes).

Try the same design in your sketchbook using different colors (look at pages 10–11 for ideas).

Add accessories to your outfit.

Use metallic marker pens to add sparkling details.

Add pockets and buttons to make your outfit more realistic.

Talk like a
FASHION DESIGNER

Designers use special words and phrases to talk about their creations. Read on to learn how to talk like a fashion designer.

Accessory
Extra item, like a necklace or bag, that can be worn with an outfit

Brand
Line of fashion products under one name

Chic
Another word for "stylish"

Color-blocking
Wearing one or more blocks of solid color in one outfit

DIY
Stands for "do it yourself"

Dyeing
Using a dye to change the color of a fabric

Embellish
Adding decoration to something

Eyewear
Fashionable glasses or sunglasses

Fashion designer
Person whose job is to come up with ideas for new clothes

Fibers
Very fine threads that make up a material

Fray
Where fabric has been worn away

Garments
Another word for clothes

Headwear
Accessory that is worn on your head, like a hat, headband, or tiara

Hemline
Folded or sewn edge of a piece of clothing

Inspiration
Something or someone that gives you ideas

Makeover
When you change your clothes or the way you look to try out a new style

Monochrome

Made up of one color

Mood board

Board of colors, textures, pictures, and things to give you inspiration

Natural

Natural materials are made from plant and animal fibers such as cotton or wool

Outline

Shape made by the edge of an outfit

Palette

Range of colors and tones that you use in your designs

Pastels

Soft shade of color, like lilac or baby pink

Pattern

Design that is repeated lots of times

Recycle

Use something instead of throwing it away

Silhouette

See **outline**

Sleepwear

Clothes that you wear to bed

Style

Overall look created by putting together clothes and accessories

Stylist

Person whose job is to put clothing and accessories together

Sustainable fashion

Clothes and accessories made without harming the environment or the people who make them

Swatch

Small piece of fabric

Synthetic

Materials that are made from chemicals by people

Texture

The way a material feels

Trend

Look or outfit that is in fashion at a particular time

Trim

Decorations that are used to make something look nicer

Upcycling

Improve something that you would normally throw away, so that it can be used again

Vintage

Fashion from past decades, such as the 1980s

Volume

Amount of space that a piece of clothing takes up

Wardrobe

Entire collection of clothes

INDEX

ACKNOWLEDGMENTS

The publisher would like to thank: Lol Johnson for photography; Richard Leeney for photography; Belle Thackray and Issy Thomson for modeling and giving interviews; Yumiko Tahata and Maria Thomson for photoshoot assistance; Bettie Capstick, Lola Capstick, Tea Cruz, Chloe Alyse Hadley, and Be Lily Hill for modeling; Jemma Battaglia and Nicola Orme at Alison Hayes for supplying samples; Amina Youssef for editorial assistance; Carrie Love for additional editorial; Molly Lattin for additional illustration; Caroline Hunt for proofreading; Hilary Bird for the index.

Lesley Ware would like to thank her mom and dad, Gwendolyn and Herbert Leslie Williams, for having such cool style to admire. She would like to thank the talented and expeditious team at DK Books! Especially Sarah Larter, Satu Fox, Joanne Clark, and Emma Hobson, with whom she had the pleasure of working the most. Also, Tiki Papier for gracing these pages with the World's Most Fashionable Paper Doll!

About the illustrator

Tiki Papier is drawn to adventure. An avid illustrator and amateur fashionista, she travels the world with her sidekick, The World's Most Fashionable Paper Doll.

On each trip, Tiki packs an enormous box of pens and a pair of tiny scissors, to make new outfits for the ever-changing, ever-stylish paper doll. From Mexico City to Paris to the corner shop, Tiki finds a world of inspiration!